espresso

Prayers

David Winter

espresso

Prayers

Perfect shots for
any time of day

LION

A Lion Book
an imprint of
Lion Hudson plc
Wilkinson House, Jordan Hill Road,
Oxford OX2 8DR, England
www.lionhudson.com
ISBN 978 0 7459 5311 3 (UK)
ISBN 978 0 8254 6268 9 (USA)

Distributed by:

UK: Marston Book Services, PO Box 269,
Abingdon, Oxon, OX14 4YN

USA: Trafalgar Square Publishing,
814 N. Franklin Street, Chicago, IL 60610

USA: Christian Market: Kregel Publications,
PO Box 2607, Grand Rapids, Michigan 49501

First edition 2008
10 9 8 7 6 5 4 3 2 1 0

Text Acknowledgments
p. 80 'I do not ask you, Lord, to rid this world of pain'
taken from *A Treasury of the Holy Spirit* by Michael
Buckley (ed), copyright © 1984 Hodder & Stoughton.

p. 89 Extract from *Common Worship: Services
and Prayers for the Church of England* copyright
© The Archbishops' Council 2000.

The text paper used in this book has been
made from wood independently certified
as having come from sustainable forests.

A catalogue record for this book is available
from the British Library

Typeset in 10/13 Baskerville BT
Printed and bound in Malta
by Gutenberg Press

Contents

Introduction

There's no doubt a good, strong coffee gives your body a bit of a surge, which is probably why more and more people treat themselves to a dose of espresso at regular intervals throughout the day. Doubtless, patterns vary, but for many of us it's one when we wake up, dispelling the drowsiness of sleep; one at breakfast, to give us a boost as we embark on the day's activities; and one mid-morning, for a re-surge of energy. Then we have one at lunchtime, another at what used to be 'tea-time', probably another after the evening meal, and one before we go to bed (not a good idea, the doctors say – liable to keep you awake!). At each point, our bodily batteries feel recharged.

Human beings are not appliances, however. We need more than the physical surge of caffeine to see us through the day peacefully and effectively. We are spiritual beings, and there can't be many people who haven't, at some time or another, felt the need for a different kind of 'boost', one that is not chemical but spiritual.

Traditionally, that has been found in prayer; but in the heady rush of modern life there seems no time for quiet reflection, closed eyes, folded hands, an empty church and all that. So, on the whole, we don't pray, but (somewhere deep down) we miss it. We have a hunch that there's more to life than work and mortgages and commuting and domestic chores. We also suspect that no amount of coffee can meet that need. So, is there a place and a possibility for prayer in modern life?

This little book claims that there is. Think of it like those coffees: little surges of renewal throughout the day. Think of it as plugging in – don't ask me how, but it works – to a Person and a power much greater than ourselves, an immense source of love and strength and hope.

Here are some 'espresso prayers' to get you started. It must at least be worth giving them a try!

Using This Book

Coffee shops offer us a bewildering range of different drinks – latte, cappuccino, Americano, double espresso, macchiato and so on. They all come under the general heading of 'coffee', but there's a great deal of difference between them.

This little book of prayers offers the same kind of variety. Some of them are ancient prayers put into modern language. Some of them are new prayers, but in the traditional style of praying. Some of them are extended reflections, arising out of the kind of situations we often find ourselves experiencing. And some, to be honest, are there to show that prayer isn't always meant to be solemn and po-faced. Believe it or not, it can be fun, especially when it invites us to laugh at our weaknesses and prejudices.

Some of the prayers you can take and make your own, word for word. Some of them offer material for your own reflection, inviting you to apply the ideas to your own situation at the moment. And some might provide a 'way in' to prayer for those who are unfamiliar, or even suspicious, of the whole idea. I hope that somewhere in this little selection you will find words, ideas or images that will help to open doors for you into the big, big world of prayer.

Prayers for Every Day

The First Cup: First Stirrings

Lord, I am alive!
There is light at the window,
the hours of darkness are over.
'Darkness and light to you are both
    alike.'
You provide the darkness for rest
and the light for activity.
As I slept, you were awake, watching
    over me.
As I wake, you are still with me, going
    before me into the new day.
My hours of sleep were yours;
now I place the hours of activity into
    your hands.
Amen.

Thank you, Lord, for bringing me
    safely to the beginning of this day.
During it, keep me from wrong and
    shield me from its dangers.
Help me to make wise choices
and guide me to do what is right,
through Jesus Christ our Lord.
Amen.
Based on the Morning Collect, *The Book of*
Common Prayer

As I wake, the troubles of the day ahead
    come rushing into my mind.
Lord, I am anxious about many things –
people, work, money.
Sometimes I feel I just can't face the new
    day.
But you are the God of forgiveness and
    new beginnings.
May this new day be the beginning for
    me of a fresh confidence
in your faithful love,
and in your power to bring healing and
    peace into my life.
Amen.

Into your hands, Lord, I place this day.
I cannot know what it holds for me, or
    for those I love.

But I can know your faithful love for
   them and for me,
and it is on this that I rest my hope and
   confidence.
Amen.

Lord God, you are the creator of the
   light.
As your sun rises this morning,
may the greatest of all lights, your love,
rise like the sun in our hearts.
Amen.
From the Armenian Apostolic Liturgy

I commit myself into your hands, Lord,
   for this day.
May your presence be with me to its
   very end.
Remind me constantly that in any good
   thing that I may do
I am simply serving you.
Give me, therefore, a diligent and
   watchful spirit –
to seek in everything to know your will,
and, when I know it, to do it gladly, to
   your glory,
through Jesus Christ our Lord.
Amen.
After the Gelasian Sacramentary

The Second Cup:
Facing the Day

Lord, you light up the minds that are
    open to you,
you are the joy of the hearts that love you
and the strength of the wills that serve you.
Today may I be so open to you
that my love for you sets me free truly
    to serve you –
because to be your servant is to be
    perfectly free,
in Jesus Christ our Lord.
Amen.
After St Augustine

Going out and coming in,
meeting old friends and colleagues and
    new ones,
wheeling and dealing, or at the work
    bench;
on the phone or at the bedside of the
    sick,
driving the car or standing in the train:
help me today to be calm, courteous,
    gentle and patient,
even when I don't want to be.
Amen.

Lord, I will probably be very busy today.
Even if, in the rush of the day, I forget
   you, please don't forget me!

Lord, work your holy will in me this day,
and work your holy will *through* me, too.
May I do something today simply for
   love of you,
something that pleases you.
In that way, when evening comes,
I shall find myself nearer to you.
Lead me today.
Above all lead me to yourself and
   surround me with your generous love.
Amen.
After Edward Pusey

I haven't the slightest idea what this day
   will bring:
pleasure or trouble, sorrow or joy,
whether I shall be happy or cast down,
whether I shall suffer pain and grief
or stride confidently through its hours.
Whatever comes, dear Lord, I place
   myself into your hands
and submit myself to your will,
consecrating the whole day to your love
   and to your greater glory.
Amen.
After St Francis Xavier

God be in my head, and in my
    understanding;
God be in my eyes, and in my looking;
God be in my mouth, and in my
    speaking;
God be in my heart, and in my thinking;
God be at my end, and at my departing.

Book of Hours, sixteenth century

Lord, you know I love the children very
    much,
but getting them off to school stretches
    my patience to breaking point.
Why do they have to argue over the
    breakfast cereal,
squabble about the lunch boxes,
lose their caps or gloves or sports gear at
    the last moment?
Are they sent to test me?
If they are, then I often fail the test.
Give me today superhuman patience,
a genuine parental smile
and a minute glimpse of what it means
    to be nine again.
Lord, you know I love the children very
    much –
almost as much, perhaps, as you do.

Amen.

I think I'm going to be late again
and it's all my fault.
As I sit here willing the traffic to move,
only just resisting the temptation to beep
    at the idiot in front
(the lights have been green for all of five
    seconds),
I know what I need is a better sense of
    perspective.
Really, five minutes won't make much of
    a difference,
but my arriving in a bad mood will spoil
    the whole day.
God of infinite time, God of infinite
    patience,
grant this tense and troubled commuter
    a little of your infinite peace.
Amen.

Lord, may I pass this day in joy and
    peace,
without stumbling and without sin;
so that when I reach the evening I may
    praise you,
the source of joy and our constant guide
    and protector.
Amen.

From the Mozarabic Liturgy

Mid-morning Break:
Pause for Reflection

Lord Jesus Christ,
I give you my hands to do your work,
my feet to walk your way,
my eyes to see as you see,
my tongue to speak your words,
my mind, so that you may shape my
    thoughts,
my spirit, that you may prompt my
    prayers.
Above all, I give you my heart,
so that in me your Father, and all
    mankind, may be loved.
I give you myself, so that it is you,
    Lord,
who live and work and pray and love in
    me.

Lancelot Andrewes

A precious moment or two to think
in the rush and bustle of the morning –
thank you, Lord, for this precious pause.
Remind me of your presence, renew me
    in body, mind and spirit,
so that the space where I am working
becomes a kind of sanctuary,
a sacred place of blessing.
Amen.

Lord, make me an instrument of your
    peace.
Where there is hatred, let me sow love;
where there is injury, let me sow pardon;
where there is doubt, let me sow faith;
where there is despair, let me give hope;
where there is darkness, let me give light;
where there is sadness, let me give joy.

Divine Master, grant that I may not try
    to be comforted, but to comfort;
not try to be understood, but to
    understand;
not try to be loved, but to love.
Because it is in giving that we are received,
it is in forgiving that we are forgiven,
and it is in dying that we are born to
    eternal life.
After St Francis of Assisi

Teach me, Lord,
how to serve you as you deserve,
to give and not to count the cost;
to fight and not to mind the wounds;
to work and not to long for rest;
to labour and not to do it for any reward
less than knowing that I am doing your
    will,
through Jesus Christ our Lord.
Amen.

After St Ignatius Loyola

Who am I, Lord?
Sometimes I wonder.
Am I mum, or dad, or grandpa or
    grandma?
Am I the accounts clerk, or the nurse,
    or the engineer?
Am I attractive, outward-going, popular?
Or am I (as I suspect), tolerated,
patronized, accepted but not really
    welcomed?
Who am I, Lord?
Because sometimes I really don't know.

But you know me.
'You know when I sit down and when
    I rise up;
you understand my thoughts before
    I think them.

Even before a word is on my tongue,
    Lord, you know it completely.'
In which case, Lord, could you let me in
    on the secret?
I don't want praise or compliments, just
    the truth.
Who am I? Am I *really* your child, deeply
    and truly loved?
Because if I am, I can put up with all the
    rest.

Lord, I don't care about wealth,
I don't care about honours,
I don't care about pleasures
or even the joys of poetry.
I only pray that during all my life I may
    have love:
that I may have pure love,
so that I may learn to love you purely.

After Chaitanya, an Indian mystic

Thank you, Lord, for all the good
   things
you have done for me:
the pains and insults you have borne for
   me.
Merciful Redeemer – my Friend and
   Brother –
may I know you more clearly,
love you more dearly,
and follow you more nearly,
day by day.
Amen.
After St Richard of Chichester

Holy Spirit,
linking me to the love of the Father and
   the Son,
you who comfort those who are being
   tested,
enter into the very depths of my heart
   and will
with the brightness of your dazzling
   light.
My soul is sometimes like a desert,
   parched and dry:
water it, I pray, with the refreshing dew
   of your grace,
making fruitful that which has long lain
   barren.

May the fiery arrows of your love
   penetrate my heart and will,
setting them on fire with such a love
that all my failure, neglect and feebleness
   may be consumed,
as your great love takes me in its
   embrace.

After St Augustine

Lunch: Refreshment

Lord, at this hour, you hung on the
    cross,
arms outstretched in blessing for the
    world.
There you spoke words of forgiveness,
there you showed us that love is stronger
    than hate.
Saviour of the world,
who by that cross and the shedding of
    your blood won us forgiveness,
save us and help us, we humbly pray.
Amen.

Like the hunted deer longing for cool
    water,
my heart longs for you –
for the refreshment of your presence.
Now, in the middle of the day,
strengthen and renew me, I pray,
so that with joy and courage I may face
    the rest of this day.
Amen.

Lord, you fed your people in the desert
  long ago
with bread from heaven.
Your Son fed the crowds with loaves and
  fish,
and you taught us to ask you for our
  daily bread.
Now, as I break my lunchtime bread,
may I see it as a sign of your love and
  care for me.
Amen.

Blessed be the Lord God of the universe
who brings forth bread from the earth to
make the hearts of people glad.
Ancient Hebrew blessing

Lord, I really don't know which
  sandwich to choose:
pastrami, prawn cocktail, smoked
  salmon, cheddar cheese, bacon, lettuce
  and tomato?
And shall I have it on white, brown,
  wholemeal or granary bread?
Lord, it's so difficult – and if I get it
  wrong I shall regret it all afternoon.

I suppose that there are many people
   who would settle for *any* sandwich
on *any* kind of bread.
They have a 'choice': food or hunger.
Help me, as I wrestle with my luxury of
   choices, to remember them –
those who have no choice but to go
   short.
And as I remember them, to do
   something about it,
for your love's sake.
Amen.

For food in a world where many
   hunger;
for faith in a world where many walk in
   fear;
for friends in a world where many walk
   alone:
I give you grateful thanks, O Lord.
Girl Guide World Hunger prayer

Lord, this hour feels like an island in
   the day's sea
or an oasis in the desert.
Help me to see it rather as part of the
   whole of my life today.
You are with me at each moment,
   whether I realize it or not:
working, laughing, resting, arguing –
my unseen Companion and constant
   Friend.
Amen.

Thank you, Father, for my food
and my lunchtime coffee.
Strengthened in body, refreshed in mind,
may I go into the rest of the day with
   renewed confidence and faith.
Amen.

Lord, your sea is so big
and my boat is so small!
Sailor's prayer

Coffee Break: Facing Pressure

I'm hoping for a phone call this
    afternoon
from someone special.
I hope they'll apologize, say they didn't
    mean it,
that it's all back on again.
It will be difficult to concentrate on
    anything else until they call –
there's nothing worse than waiting for
    the phone to ring,
or when it does, finding the wrong
    person's on the line.
But I feel I should hold out –
after all, it wasn't my fault, I didn't start it.
Though I suppose I could end it by
    picking up the phone
and saying 'sorry' myself.
Would that be weakness… or strength?
I think it's over to you, Lord.

Lord, I want to pray for those I work
    with,
people I see every day,
spend many hours with.
I didn't choose them,
and they didn't choose me,

but life, or the management, has thrown
    us together.
Some I like.
(Perhaps one or two I like too much.)
Some I am indifferent to.
Some – a few – I find very difficult.
This isn't like spending time with my
    friends;
more like being trapped on a desert
    island with a cross-section of humanity.
Some are coarse, some laugh a lot,
some never laugh at all,
and some are always whingeing about
    something.
There they are, though, and you have
    put me among them.
I'm sure I get on the nerves of some of
    my colleagues,
particularly those who don't like me at all.
There's one person who's in a position to
    make my life miserable,
and they do.

Teach me, Lord, to learn to live with
    them all,
to see each as of infinite value to you.
And though I prefer this one or that one,
to recognize that where people are
    concerned, you have no favourites.
Amen.

At three o'clock in the afternoon
Jesus died on the cross.
Father, at this hour, may the reminder of
   his death for me
reawaken both my love for you
and sorrow at the memory of my sins
   that needed such forgiveness.
Amen.

It's time to fetch the children from
   school –
to join the mothers at the gates, waiting
   and watching
for that familiar little face to appear.
It may be laughing, or cross, or sulky,
but I don't really mind,
because I know that when we meet it will
   be all right.
I suppose, Lord, that's a bit how you feel
   about us,
as we make our way to meet you.
We may be laughing, or angry, or
   resentful.
But when you welcome us we know, in
   some deep way, that all will be well.
Amen.

Lord of the loving heart,
may mine be loving, too.
Lord of the gracious lips,
may mine be gracious, too.
Lord of the gentle hands,
may mine be gentle, too.
May my thoughts and words and actions
    bear witness
to the One I seek to follow,
Jesus Christ, my Lord.
Amen.

God, you are the author of peace
and the lover of concord.
To know you is eternal life,
to serve you is perfect freedom.
Defend your children from everything
    that evil and temptation can throw at
    them,
so that – trusting in your help –
they may not fear anything or anybody,
through Jesus Christ our Lord.
Amen.

Adapted from *The Book of Common Prayer*

Eternal God,
who in your gentle love for the human
    race
sent your Son to be our Saviour;

to take upon him our nature
and to suffer death on the cross for us:
may we follow the example of his
    patience and humility
and also share in his risen life;
through Jesus Christ our Lord.
Amen.

Adapted from *The Book of Common Prayer*

Give me, Lord,
a humble, quiet, peaceful, patient, tender
    and generous mind,
and in all my thoughts, words and deeds
    a taste of the Holy Spirit.
Give me, Lord, a lively faith, a firm
    hope, a fervent generosity
and a deep love for you.
Take from me anything that is lukewarm
    in my devotion,
anything that is dull in my life of prayer.
Give me gratitude in thinking of you and
    of your goodness to me.
And then, Lord, give me the grace to
    work hard for the things for which I
    pray!
Through Jesus Christ our Lord.
Amen.

After a prayer of St Thomas More

I think I've lost the treatment file
and the staff nurse will be round shortly.
Of course, I haven't actually *lost* it.
I mean, it hasn't disappeared into thin
    air.
It's just nowhere I can lay my hands on
    it,
and bed nine is buzzing for something.
I'm due off at five, but if I can't find the
    file
I won't be able to go until it's found.
I believe there's a patron saint for lost
    things, or is it lost causes?
Well, whoever he or she is, please get to
    work right now.
Perhaps I'd do better to say a little
    prayer myself –
calm myself down.
Lord, I need your help, and quickly.
At least you know where I put it – they
    tell me you know everything,
and this is just a silly little detail.
I do tend to panic when things like this
    happen:
help me to stay calm.
I think I should cancel the buzzer and
    see what bed nine wants –
oh, here's the blessed file, right next to
    the button.
Thank you, Lord, or saint whoever-it-is!

May my work be a joy
because it is done in your Name;
may my labour be fruitful,
because you, Lord, give the increase;
may my presence be a blessing, not a
    hindrance, to those with whom I work,
and may this day, and every day, be
    special
because it is your gift.
Amen.

The Sixth Cup:
Family, Home, Friends

Eternal God, whose son Jesus shared at
  Nazareth
the joys of family and home;
bless my home, my family, those very
  dear to me,
and those to whom I am dear.
As we gather at the end of the working
  day,
may your Spirit draw us closer,
in love for one another and for you.
Amen.

Bless my children, heavenly Father,
with healthy bodies and lively minds,
with the Spirit's graces and gifts,
with pleasant dispositions and good
  habits.
Guard them in body, mind and spirit
and keep them close to your heart.
Amen.

After Jeremy Taylor

I thank you, Lord, for the one
who shares my life,
puts up with my moods,
forgives my failures, cares for those
    I care about –
the companion of my days and the
    sharer of my deepest thoughts.
This is love:
and you have said that those who live
    in love live in you,
and you live in them.
So thank you, Father, for the one who
    makes your love real to me,
for your love's sake.
Amen.

Home is such a lovely idea
that you, Lord, must have invented it.
It's the place where we can be ourselves,
laugh and argue and tease and cry –
where we can do nothing, creatively,
without feeling guilty.
Thank you for my home:
our home here on earth,
and the one you've prepared for us in
    heaven.
Amen.

Some of those I love are far away:
for work, for holidays, for gap years
or because they've made their home
   there.
I miss them, sometimes very much,
but I know that though they are out of
   my sight
they are still in yours.
Hold them in your love, Lord,
and help me to see that distance alone
   cannot destroy love.
They are yours, and I am yours,
and that is permanent and binding.
Amen.

Give me, Lord, a heart
that no unworthy thought can drag down;
an unconquered heart, which no trial can
   wear out;
an upright heart, which cannot be led
   astray by corrupt motives.
More than that, Lord, give me
   understanding, so that I can know you
   better;
perseverance in seeking you;
wisdom, to find you;
and a faith that will cling to you for ever,
through Jesus Christ our Lord.
Amen.
After St Thomas Aquinas

Lord, make the door of this house so
    wide
that any who are looking for friendship,
    love and care can find it here;
so narrow that envy, pride and hatred
    are shut out.
May its threshold be so smooth that no
    one, young or old, stumbles at its
    entrance,
but rough enough to daunt the tempter's
    power.
Lord, make the door of this simple house
    a gateway to the kingdom of heaven.
Amen.
After Thomas Ken

I don't think dad knows who I am any
    more:
he's got steadily worse, living in a little
    world of his own,
full of distant memories, but unaware
    what day it is,
or even that it's his daughter who's
    giving him grapes.
It's like sitting next to a working model
    of someone who used to be my dad –
who played tennis with me in the
    garden, took me on outings,
helped me build sandcastles at the
    seaside.

This is the man, too, who used to sit by
   my bed and help me say my prayers,
who could do my maths homework, who
   looked so proud at my graduation.
Jesus called God 'Father', so I expect he
   knows how I feel –
having a father, and not having one, at
   the same time.
I don't think dad knows who I am any
   more,
but I know who he is, and that's all that
   matters.
Heavenly Father, help me to keep very
   close to my earthly one,
particularly now.
Amen.

Evening: Relaxation

Now at last it's time to relax,
put my feet up, watch TV, read the
     paper.
The children are in bed, the day's work
     is over,
it's quiet outside and inside,
and my heart is quiet, too.
There's not really even any need to
     think,
certainly not to worry:
'The day's troubles are enough for the
     day,' said Jesus.

This is my favourite time of the day,
but only because the past hours have
     been full of people and work and
     activity.
I suppose this is the 'sabbath' of the day,
the time for rest and renewal.
So, as I sit, feet up, half asleep, renew me
     in mind, body and spirit, Lord.

Lord, support us all the day long
of this troubled life;
until the evening comes,
the busy world is hushed,
the fever of life is over
and our day is done.
Then, Lord, in your mercy, grant us
quiet rest, safe lodging, and peace at the
     last,
through Jesus Christ our Lord.
Amen.
John Henry Newman

Light of joy,
poured out in holy glory by the eternal
     Father,
holy and blessed Jesus Christ,
the Light of the world:
as we come to sunset and the lights of
     evening begin to shine,
I praise you, Father, Son and Holy Spirit.
And I worship you, Son of God,
Light of our life,
joining my voice to the songs of the
     whole creation.
Evening hymn of the ancient Greek Church

Darkness falls outside:
indoors the lights are switched on,
    creating another light –
not the light of the sun, nor even of the
    moon,
but the light of human enterprise and
    invention.
Many people make that welcome light
    possible:
those who discovered and harnessed
    electricity to our use;
those who man the power stations and
    service the grid;
those who maintain it in flood, gale and
    storm.
Help me, Lord, not to take it, or them,
    for granted –
light at the touch of a finger,
banishing the darkness of nature.
And remind me that my inner darkness,
my negative thoughts, my bitter feelings,
    my life of self,
cannot be so easily illumined.
Shine your light into my heart, Lord,
    and by that divine light
turn my night into day.
Amen.

Lord, every holy motive,
every good thought and every positive
  action
comes from you.
Give me, and all your people, that peace
  which the world can't give.
It will set my heart free to do what you
  require,
it will protect me from every fear,
it will enable me to live my life in
  serenity and peace,
through Jesus Christ our Lord.
Amen.

After the Evening Collect, *The Book of Common*
Prayer

Lord, let my prayer rise before you like
  incense
and the lifting up of my hands like the
  evening sacrifice.
Amen.

The Last Cup:
Wiping the Slate Clean

It's been a pretty average day:
I lost my temper twice
(once with the kids, once with a motorist
  at the traffic lights);
I told one lie
and disguised the truth four or five
  times;
I definitely envied the boss his new car;
and there was a bit of flirting over the
  water cooler.
Then I took the last vegetarian lunch,
  even though I'm not a vegetarian
(it looked much nicer than the cottage
  pie) –
and the woman from reception, who is
  strictly veggie, had bread and cheese
  instead.
Then, Lord, I haven't thought of you
  since I gabbled my prayers before
  breakfast
(I was already five minutes behind
  schedule).
So, one way or another, as I come to the
  day's end
'average' is probably a euphemism.

I'm not proud of myself today,
and I offer no excuses.
All I can do is ask you to forgive me,
to wipe my slate clean at the end of the
   day,
and to help me to do better tomorrow –
not because I deserve it, but because
   Jesus died for my forgiveness.
Amen.

God of mercy,
Father of Jesus,
I confess that I have sinned today in
   thought, word and deed.
I have not loved you or others with my
   whole heart.
Please forgive what I have been,
help me to amend what I am,
and direct what I shall be in the future;
so that I may act justly,
love mercy,
and walk humbly with you, my God.
Amen.

Adapted from *Common Worship*

Be present, merciful God,
and protect us through the silent hours
   of this night,
that we who are wearied by the changes
   and chances of this fleeting world
may rest on your eternal changelessness,
through Jesus Christ our Lord.
Amen.

From the Leonine Sacramentary

Watch, dear Lord,
with those who wake or watch or weep
   tonight,
and give your angels charge over those
   who sleep.
Care for those who are ill,
give rest to those who are weary,
bless those who are dying,
comfort those who suffer,
and rejoice with those who are joyous:
and all for your love's sake.
Amen.

Adapted from St Augustine

Visit, Lord, this house and family
    tonight,
and drive from it everything that is evil.
May your holy angels dwell under its
    roof to keep us in peace,
and let your blessing always be on us.
Amen.

Save us, Lord, while we are awake,
and guard us while we are asleep,
that waking we may watch with Christ,
and sleeping may rest in peace.
Amen.
Roman Breviary

Goodnight, stars,
goodnight, moon;
goodnight, children,
goodnight, my loved one.
Goodnight, my soul.
May we rest in peace tonight.
Amen.

Prayers for Special Occasions

The Expectant Mother

Inside me, deep in the core of my being,
there is another life –
a very precious one,
which will profoundly change and enrich
   me over the years.
I can feel its movements, and the
   midwife can hear its heartbeat.
This tiny life depends as utterly and
   completely on me
as I do on you, Lord.
I've wanted to be a mother.
I love children.

But this isn't just 'a child'.
This is my son or daughter, our child,
a third person in our home and our lives.
I can feel the burden of responsibility:
Will I be up to it? Will I let this little life
    down? Will I be a good mother?
We call you 'Father' and look to you as
    our heavenly parent.
I pray that you, who hold to your breast
    all your earthly children,
will hold me and help me to be everything
    my 'expected' child will need.
Amen.

A Christening

The parents' prayer

She looks so little,
tiny pink hands sticking out of the
   christening robe
that was once mine, long ago.
We've already welcomed her into our
   home,
a fully-fledged member of our family.
Now, here in church, we are welcoming
   her as part of the family of God,
his loved child for all eternity.
'Christ claims you for his own,' says the
   vicar,
as he makes the sign of the cross on her
   little forehead –
a mark of suffering and death for you,
   Lord,
but of life and hope for her.
Everyone's here – proud grandparents,
   smiling friends, uncles and aunts,
real and honorary.
It's her first public occasion,
a proud moment for us.
Help us, gentle Lord, to be worthy of
   her trust –
and yours.
Amen.

The godparent's prayer

It was good of them to ask me
and I was touched by it.
Yes, I'd like to be his godparent –
but what does that mean?
You know, Lord, that I'm not exactly
   pious,
but I want to do this job well,
not just because they're my friends,
but because I think children growing up
   in the modern world
need all the help they can get –
ours, and yours, Lord.
They told me I should pray for him,
and I will, I promise, every day.
It's a long journey, life, with some funny
   twists and turns.
If my prayers can help him on his way
(onwards and upwards, as we say at work),
then so much the better.
Amen.

For the parents and godparents

Father, may the love, prayers, faith and
   example
of parents and godparents
be a constant support on this child's
   journey of faith;

until, guided and supported by them,
this faith becomes his/her own,
through Jesus Christ our Lord.
Amen.

For a special needs child

We feel very humbled, Lord,
that you have entrusted us with such a
     special child.
We realize what patience we shall need
and how our love, at times, may be tested
     to the limits.
Help us to value this precious child as
     you do,
to rejoice in every little sign of progress,
to be generous with praise and gentle in
     correction;
so that she/he may grow up secure and
     loved,
enriching our lives and the lives of
     others,
through Jesus Christ our Lord.
Amen.

A Child's Birthday

They'll all be excited and noisy,
eager to get at the food and win the
  games.
And there, bobbing about among them,
is our little child –
but one year older.
Lord, what lies ahead?
Life seems so scary nowadays, so
  unpredictable:
what sort of a world awaits these children
  as they grow up?
We can love and protect them now,
but not always, as you, Lord, can.
Please guard and guide this young life
  for ever.
That's our prayer.
Amen.

A Wedding

The bride's prayer

Everyone says it's my 'big day',
but at the moment I'm feeling sick with
    panic, Lord.
It's not that I don't love him (you know
    that I do),
but it just seems such a huge step –
and in front of crowds of people, too.
I might start to stutter,
lose my veil, trip up my dad – even faint.
Perhaps what I should do is concentrate
    on *being* married
rather than on *getting* married.
After all, tomorrow the wedding will be
    over,
but the marriage will only just be
    starting.
So be with us, Lord,
now, at the start of things,
and then all through the years that lie
    ahead.
Amen.

The bridegroom's prayer

What do I pray for on my wedding day?
Love – but we've got that already: that it
    may grow over the years.
Faithfulness – to one another, and to the
    promises we shall make today.
Honesty – to mean what I say and to say
    what I mean.
Thoughtfulness – because sometimes I
    don't realize the pain and hurt I'm
    causing her.
Courage – because sometimes things will
    be difficult.
All of that, Lord, and because I'm me,
    and not some plaster saint,
all the help you can give me now
and until we are parted by death.
Amen.

Lord Jesus, you were a guest
at a wedding in Cana, long ago.
There was a crisis: the wine ran out.
Your answer was to transform ordinary
    water into rich, red wine.
Today, please take two ordinary people
and by your presence with them
turn 'ordinary' lives into treasure houses
    of your love.
Amen.

The two will become one:
that's what the Bible says.
'Forsaking all others...'
but clinging to each other
as long as we both shall live.
A strange sort of arithmetic there, Lord:
one plus one equals one.

Lord, may this marriage be life-giving
    and life-long,
made all the richer because you are at
    the heart of it,
giving strength and grace.
May they bring comfort and confidence
    to each other
through their mutual love and loyalty.
God of love, hear our prayer.
Amen.

Adapted from *Common Worship*

May their home be a place of hospitality
where all are welcome,
and no one in need or distress is turned
    away.
Generous God, hear our prayer.
Amen.

Adapted from *Common Worship*

Lord, may their children
be cared for with devotion and love.
May they watch them grow in body,
   mind and spirit,
hearts content and joyfully confident in
   life,
and in your promise of an eternal home
   in heaven.
Amen.

A New Home

Lord Jesus, you shared the life of an
    earthly home.
Bless this house.
May it be to those who live in it
a haven of security, peace and love;
and for all who visit it
a place of welcome and warmth.
Amen.

I know it's only bricks, mortar, wood
    and tiles,
but it feels at the moment lonely and
    unloved.
This was someone's home –
their children played in the garden,
they slept in the bedroom, washed in the
    bathroom,
cooked in the kitchen.
But now it's ours, though it doesn't quite
    feel ours yet.
It's our furniture. Soon our pictures will
    be on the walls,
our dirty boots in the porch.

That will help, but what will help most
     of all is when this house
(three bedrooms, two reception rooms,
     central heating and nice garden)
becomes our home.
Builders make houses; you, Lord, make
     homes:
please make one here.

Going on Holiday

Soon we'll be packing the car
and then it's off for that blissful
   fortnight:
sun, sand and sea.
The children have been excited for
   weeks,
but to be honest I'm a bit anxious.
Travelling always seems to have its
   problems –
a breakdown somewhere I can't speak
   the language;
one of the children getting ill;
losing the passports, or the tickets, or the
   credit cards.
Yet we call it a 'holiday' –
a 'holy' time of rest and relaxation.
Help me, Lord, not to let sensible
   precautions become anxious cares,
to remember that these will be 'holy'
   days if you are with us,
which, of course, you are.
Amen.

Lord, you led your people long ago
across the Red Sea to the promised land;
you led the wise men by a star to the
    infant Jesus.
Well, we're only going to Blackpool,
but please be with us as we travel.
Keep us safe, and bring us in the end
to our promised destination.
Amen.

Fleeing the Nest

The fledgling's prayer

Today, Lord, I'm leaving home.
It's a strange feeling, because this has
    been my place of safety,
the door through which I've always
    returned to the security of the familiar –
my room, my bits and pieces, my
    family.

But now I'm leaving, and perhaps I'll
    never live here again.
It's a huge step, and although I want to
    move on, I feel the tug of tearing roots.
Of course I'll come back.
Those I love most in all the world are
    here.
But I'll come back an independent
    person, a visitor,
someone who comes and goes.
It's odd and rather frightening, but also
    exciting.
Come with me, Lord, on this next part of
    my journey.
Amen.

The parents' prayer

So the nest is going to be empty.
For eighteen years we've known this
    would come one day,
but it doesn't make it any easier.
The car will go to the station, loaded
    with bags and things,
and tonight there'll be a phone call:
'I'm here. It's great. I've met the guy in
    the next room and he's really cool.'
And we shall worry, and pray, and
    worry…

It's not as though we didn't know it
    would happen,
it's just that suddenly the house will be
    empty and silent.
I shall keep a bed made up in the spare
    room –
you never know when it might be
    needed.

Lord, we don't want to be clinging
    parents,
and we're genuinely glad that everything
    has worked out so well –
exams, applications, courses, loans.
We'll get used to it, I suppose, and find
    other things
to talk about and worry about.

Help us now, though, because I think we
   both feel, well, almost bereaved,
and it hurts!
Amen.

Going to a Funeral

I'm afraid, Lord, to be honest:
afraid of losing control of my emotions,
afraid of the way my life will have to
   change,
and afraid that one day I won't be in the
   pew but in the coffin myself.
You shed tears at the grave of your
   friend,
yet without fear, without distress,
because you could see beyond the tomb
   and the tears,
knowing that life is stronger than death.
So help me, Lord, to trust you in the
   darkness as well as in the light,
and bring me through today to a place of
   hope and faith again.
Amen.

Before an Interview

I keep looking in the mirror, Lord,
and all I see is a worried face and a nasty
spot on my chin.
Surely I won't lose the job because of a
spot?
No, more likely because I'll either dry up
completely or, worse still,
just keep on talking and talking.
You know I want it… need it,
and I know I've got the qualifications
and the experience.
Apparently all I have to do is impress
them with my confidence,
personality and leadership potential.
But I'm not a good performer, am I?
And I'm not very confident, either.
So now, averting my eyes from that
frightened face in the mirror,
please, Lord, be with me.
Help me not even to try to be someone
else
(big, bouncy, confident, nature's winner)
but just be myself – the person you
made me.
Because, after all, if they don't want the
real me
they'll not find much good in the bogus
one, will they?

Facing an Exam

Help me, Lord, to do my best.
I don't demand success or honours or
   awards:
just that I may use to the full the skills
   and knowledge I have,
remembering always that they, too, are
   your gifts to me.
Help me to concentrate,
to keep calm,
to remember things;
but above all to know that it's not the
   end of the world if I fail.
Amen.

Breaking Up

I didn't want it to be like this:
angry words, hurt and tears,
   recriminations.
If it had to end, why couldn't we do it
   the gentle way –
gratitude for laughs and fun in the past,
shared memories and echoes of familiar
   songs?
I'm sorry, Lord:
sorry for my own selfishness and pride,
sorry for the angry words I spoke,
sorry that I didn't say 'thanks for the
   good times'.
And yes, all right, I'll phone and say so,
and not add anything that sounds like
   blame or scoring a point.
Lord, you invented love: you *are* love.
Help those who, for whatever reason,
   have somehow lost it.
Amen.

Making Up

It's quite hard to say sorry –
to admit that I was at fault,
to say out loud that I've been a fool
and almost lost the most precious thing
   in my life.
But help me to do it, Lord.
Forgive me my faults, I pray,
and I promise that I will try very hard
   not to remember anyone else's.
You are the God of reconciliation,
who sent your Son to bring people back
   to you and to one another.
Look at us, who handle these things so
   clumsily, with patience,
and by the mystery of love heal the hurts
   and bind up the wounds,
for Jesus Christ's sake.
Amen.

Friends and Neighbours

To love those who love us should be
   easy,
but sometimes it's not.
To love the stranger I meet, or the
   person who happens to live next door,
is more of a challenge.
To love them as you do, Lord, with
   perfect charity and compassion,
is the ultimate test of grace.
Give me that grace, Lord,
so that I can truly love and be loved.
Amen.

Being Forty

Lord, I'm forty today.
I know they've got a bit of a party planned,
and I'll get all those stupid cards about
    being 'over the hill',
and someone will welcome me to the
    Sanatogen Club
or offer to get me some Viagra.
I could really do without it,
because I know, without their jokes,
that I'm just about at the halfway mark
and I don't seem to have much to show
    for it.
I suppose this is a time to take stock,
to look at myself and ask a few questions.

Lord, there *must* be more to life than this:
forty years that have sped by,
leaving me a bit overweight, a touch
    baggy round the eyes,
but otherwise not bad (as they say) 'for
    my age'.
I realize that life is a precious gift, and I
    don't want to waste it,
so can we make this birthday a wake-up
    call for a new day?
Because being forty makes you realize
    that time's an expendable commodity.
Amen.

Being Sixty

Today, Lord, I'm sixty:
I retire, get my pension and my bus pass.
I'm what they used to call an 'old age
    pensioner',
but now, more kindly, a 'senior citizen'.
So my working life is over, and all the
    identity that went with it.
'What do you do?' people will ask me at
    parties,
and I'll have to say, 'I'm retired.'
They'll be polite, say things like 'Lucky
    you',
but they won't mean it.
Of course, I'll be able to spend more
    time with the family,
and in the garden and on the golf
    course.
I'll get under my partner's feet all the
    time
and the house (perfectly adequate
    yesterday) will seem too small.
On the other hand, I'll also have time to
    do something useful, I suppose –
to develop hidden talents, get involved in
    the life of the community,
volunteer for some of those jobs they're
    always going on about.

Lord, I'm not yet ready for the easy
  chair and the carpet slippers.
Please take whatever time I have, and
  give it meaning and purpose and
  vitality:
then I really won't mind being sixty!
Amen.

The Young and the Old

Lord, the eyes of the young see visions,
and the minds of the old dream dreams;
help us, young and old, to value the
   visions and cherish the dreams.
May the young respect the old;
may those who are older look with
   patience on the young,
so that both young and old may work
   together
for the coming of your kingdom.
Amen.

An Old Person's Prayer

Deep down, Lord, young people
  frighten me.
I don't like the way they dress, the way
  they talk,
the way they hang about on the
  pavements.
It wasn't like that when I was their age.
We were taught to respect older people,
  not to make fun of them
or frighten them.

On the other hand, the youngsters I
  know well, like my grandchildren,
seem very nice.
Perhaps my fear is actually ignorance.
If it is, then you'll have to help me:
help me not to judge too hastily,
not to let things like clothes and noise
  and nose-studs distort that judgment.
Jesus seemed to like children and young
  people.
Perhaps you could help me follow his
  example.
Amen.

A Young Person's Prayer

Old people freak me out, Lord.
They're so weird: awful clothes, no sense
 of humour,
always going 'tut-tut' and muttering
 about us.
Can't they just lighten up and stop going
 on about 'when I was your age'?

On the other hand, my gran and
 grandpa are alright.
They treat me and my friends like
 human beings,
ask what I've been doing, laugh at my
 stories,
and even seem to like my friends.
If every old person were like them...
but perhaps they are – it's just I've never
 got to know them.
So help me, Lord, to be a bit more
 patient,
a bit less critical, a bit more friendly
and not to judge people until I know
 what makes them tick.

Facing Illness

Lord, it isn't just the pain and
    discomfort
but the feeling of being useless that really
    hurts.
I don't think of myself as an invalid,
I just don't feel 'myself'.
Suddenly, I'm someone else,
someone who gets ill, needs help,
can't do things, looks pathetic.
Of course I'd like you to make me well
    again,
but I'd also like you to make me *better*:
better at being patient (instead of being
    'a patient');
better at being grateful and content;
better at accepting how I am.
Then I can place myself totally into your
    hands
and leave my worries and frustrations
    there.
Amen.

Lord Jesus, you understand suffering.
You suffered on the cross,
you wept at the grave of a dear friend.
By your suffering you transform our
    sufferings,
opening up a path of life through the
    valley of darkness
and a place of hope in the garden of
    tears.
Transform, I pray, this suffering now,
by the power of your own.
Amen.

Lord, the one I love is ill.
It's so hard to watch them suffer,
to feel helpless when they need me most.
With all my heart I pray for their
    healing,
but also that in the midst of this fear and
    anxiety
our love may be secure,
our trust in you absolute,
our eternal hope founded on the rock of
    your faithfulness,
through Jesus Christ our Lord.
Amen.

Let nothing disturb me,
nothing dismay me;
all things are passing,
God never changes.
Patient endurance
achieves what it strives for;
those who have God
find they lack nothing.
God alone satisfies.

Teresa of Avila

I do not ask you, Lord,
to rid this world of pain,
but that my pain may be free from waste,
unfretted by rebellion against your will,
unsoiled by selfishness,
purified by love of others,
and ennobled by the vision of your love,
through Jesus Christ our Lord.
Amen.

After Robert Nash

For healing

Heavenly Father,
through your Son Jesus,
who healed the sick and gave them new
    life,
make (the one I pray for) whole
in body, mind and spirit,
to your glory.
Amen.

Bring us, O Lord, at our last awakening
into the house and gate of heaven,
to enter into that gate and dwell in that
    house
where there shall be no darkness nor
    dazzling,
but one equal music;
no noise nor silence, but one equal
    possession;
no ends nor beginnings, but one equal
    eternity
in the habitations of your glory and
    dominion,
world without end.
Amen.

John Donne

Going into Hospital

Everyone says, 'It's nothing, nowadays…
just like having a tooth out.'
But the fact is, Lord, I'm scared – not
  witless, not paralyzed by it,
but I find it keeps creeping into my
  mind,
especially at night.
Someone is going to put me to sleep,
and while I'm unconscious they're going
  to operate.
When I wake up (if I wake up) I know I
  shall feel better,
but it's not an experience I'd choose to
  have.
So, Lord, calm my mind,
take control of my fertile imagination.
Walk with me into the hospital and all
  through the whole business,
even – especially – when I'm unconscious
and I don't know what's going on.
Thankfully, Lord, you do.

For Those We Have Loved
but See No Longer

Lord, they are so much more than a
  memory,
those we have dearly loved but see no
  longer.
They are still part of us, part of our lives,
their presence still pervades the home
  and the old familiar places.
They are yours, and you gave them to us
  for a season,
and for that we are grateful.
Now we hold them in your eternal love,
until that day when we shall share
  together
in the glorious light and life of your
  heavenly kingdom.
Amen.

Give rest, O Christ, to your servants
  with the saints,
where sorrow and pain are no more,
nor sighing, but life everlasting.
Russian Kontakion for the dead

For the death of a child

When I get to heaven, if I do,
the first question I shall ask is, 'Why?'
Why give us this precious little one, so
    full of promise and possibilities,
why let us dream dreams about their
    future,
make plans, shower our love on them, if –
suddenly, horribly, unbelievably – they
    are to be snatched away from us?
Somebody said to us, 'Jesus took them.'
Well, if he did, I wish he'd give them
    back.
It's very hard to pray when I feel like
    this:
angry, baffled, confused, numb.
Are there answers, Lord? Or only
    questions?

Someone else told me that you love our
    little one
even more than we do.
If that's true, then hold them fast in your
    love
until we can hold them once again in
    ours.
And comfort us, because at the moment
    the emptiness is unbearable.
Amen.